HOW TO
FOLLOW UP
WITH YOUR
NETWORK
MARKETING
PROSPECTS

Turn *"Not Now"*
Into *"Right Now"*

KEITH & TOM "BIG AL" SCHREITER

For information, contact:

Fortune Network Publishing
PO Box 890084
Houston, TX 77289 USA

Telephone: +1 (281) 280-9800

ISBN: 1-892366-42-8

ISBN-13: 978-1-892366-42-9

DEDICATION

This book is dedicated to network marketers everywhere.

I travel the world 240+ days each year. Let me know if you want me to stop in your area and conduct a live Big Al training.

http://www.BigAlSeminars.com

Get 7 mini-reports of amazing, easy sentences that create new, hot prospects.

Sign up today at:
http://www.BigAlReport.com

Other great Big Al Books available at:
http://www.BigAlBooks.com

TABLE OF CONTENTS

PREFACE

We hear our prospects say:

- "I have to think it over."
- "Now isn't the right time."
- "I am really busy."
- "Not now. Maybe later."

Of course our prospects could be politely telling us that they are not interested, but they are prospects, aren't they? So certainly they are interested in opportunity, but something is holding them back.

Are they afraid to make the decision too quickly? Are they uncomfortable with us? Was the presentation overwhelming?

Whatever the reason for delay, we must follow up with our prospects.

Follow-up doesn't have to be scary. We don't have to feel guilty or nervous. We don't have to suffer through the pain of prospects that avoid our calls.

Proper follow-up means we have great conversations with our prospects. Our prospect looks forward to our call. We are always in rapport. And when the time is right for our prospects, we are there.

Sound like fun?

Use the techniques in this book to move your prospects forward, from "not now" to "right now."

— Tom "Big Al" Schreiter

Myth or incompetency?

"The average sale or decision takes seven visits by a salesman."

Really???

I don't know if that is true. Maybe it is just a myth to keep salespeople optimistic after hearing "No!" from the same prospect after multiple harassments.

We know there are two types of prospects.

First, there are prospects who buy right away. Why?

#1. Perfect timing.

Maybe the timing is so good that the prospect has to make a decision right away. For example, the prospect falls down and hurts his knee. We sell a pain solution. How awesome is that?

Or, the doctor tells the prospect, "Lose weight now!" And we just happen to sell a diet solution.

Or better yet. The boss yells at our prospect, the prospect's co-worker trims his toenails at work, and now the prospect is stuck in commuter traffic ... our prospect is ready to act now. Yes, timing is everything!

#2. Perfect rapport.

We know our prospect, and we have perfect rapport with our prospect. It is easy to make an instant decision with someone you trust. Prospects will buy from and join with a person they trust.

However, if our prospect doesn't believe us, or doesn't trust us, nothing is going to happen. The offer can be the greatest offer in the world, but when we don't feel comfortable with a salesman, we will delay our final decision as long as possible.

Professional network marketers constantly work on improving their rapport techniques. Instant "Yes" decisions are fun to get.

Unfortunately, when we first start our network marketing career, we don't have great skills. There is a lot to learn, and we won't master everything on our first day.

Second, there are prospects who don't join or buy right away. Why?

#1. Bad timing.

Our offer could be perfect, but the prospect's circumstances could be awful. Do these examples of bad timing sound familiar?

* Loss of job. Our prospect is completely focused on survival and finding another job to pay the bills. We are an unnecessary distraction at this moment.

* Overtime at work. There's not much time for life when the employer takes up every waking hour.

* Moving. The second most stressful event in one's life. No time to humor a salesman and sit down for a presentation.

* Family issues. When our children have problems in their lives, our attention is on fixing those problems. Coming to a follow-up meeting or webinar is far down on our list of priorities.

* Relationship difficulties. Lots of drama and no time to think about our offer.

More about bad timing later. Let's look at the next reason prospects delay.

#2. Distractions.

Our prospects might get distracted with an email alert and forget to go to our web page. Or worse, there is an incoming telephone call, an urgent request from a child, or the doorbell rings. Your offer quickly fades into the background, never to be considered again.

#3. Bad sales presentation.

The prospect needed our product or service, but our presentation was amateur and awful. Maybe we committed one of these presentation sins that distanced us from our prospect:

- We read a PowerPoint presentation or flip chart to our prospect like the prospect was reading-impaired. Boring.
- We showed the prospect a commercial video. If our prospect can't stand to watch a 30-second

commercial on television, forcing our prospect to watch a 10-minute company commercial might be deadly.

- We told the prospect all about us, our facts, our awesomeness, our company history, our life history, and never once concentrated on our prospect's needs.
- We sent our prospect away to a web page. That is going to take a lot of time away from our prospect's day.
- We used an amateur high-pressure close that offended our prospect.

#4. Bad skills.

Let's say you boarded an airplane and the pilot said, "Welcome aboard. I don't know how to fly this plane, but I have a great attitude and I am motivated."

Would you get on that plane? Of course not.

Prospects can smell incompetency. If we are unpracticed and unsure, prospects will avoid doing business with us. Prospects are desperate for someone to follow, but only want to follow someone who knows where he or she is going, and has the **skills** to get there. Not many prospects are ready to jump on an incompetency mission.

Let's focus on what we can control
so that we can get "Yes" decisions.

While we can't control the bad timing in our prospect's life (Reason #1) and distractions (Reason #2), we can at least control our presentation (Reason #3) and mastery of our skills (Reason #4).

What can we do if we come across the prospect who doesn't say "Yes" right away? This is when our follow-up begins.

If we have built "Instant Trust, Belief, Influence, and Rapport!" – then follow-up will be easy. By having good rapport on our first contact with prospects, they will **look forward** to our second contact. We won't have unanswered voicemail messages or people refusing to acknowledge our other follow-up attempts.

· Unless there is future communication, all hope is gone.

When we follow up with prospects, what are they really unsure about? What holds them back?

Here is the follow-up secret that will make the difference.

Prospects don't understand everything about our business. And they won't understand any business fully until they have experienced the business for a while.

Prospects are desperate to change their lives. What prospects are really looking for is a trusted path and a trusted guide for their future success. They want to know if:

1.   You know **where** you are going.

2.   You know **how** to get there.

3.   You have the **skills** to teach them how to get there also.

So focus on the real issue. Build that trust and rapport with your prospects, and then show them that your skills will get them to their desired success.

**For now, let's assume that our sales presentation
and skills are adequate.**

Now what? That leaves "timing" as the issue.

What happens in the average day of our prospect? How does follow-up help to gradually change the prospect from a "No" to a "Yes" decision?

Let's look at the three effects of follow-up:

1. Repetition.

2. Sorting.

3. Moving parade.

The "billboard repetition" effect.

This is how repetition works in follow-up.

Let's say that five days a week I drive to the gym to work out. Same route every time. I pass the dentist, the dry cleaner, the coffee shop and the same five billboards. Unless there is something out of the ordinary, I don't even remember the drive.

One day while returning from the gym, a billboard appeared for a brand-new Italian restaurant. I love Italian food. And after working out, I am hungry!

But the timing? Well, bad timing. I had another appointment to get to.

The next day, while coming home from the gym, I remembered the Italian restaurant billboard. This time I noticed that their specialty was wood-fired oven pizza. My stomach growled with anticipation.

But this weekend's schedule was filled with errands and activities. Again the timing didn't work out.

By now, the billboard had faded away in the automatic drive to the gym. A few days later I was reminded of the Italian restaurant. Why? Because I found a door hanger flyer on my front door. It was the new Italian restaurant, advertising its wood-fired oven pizzas. I quickly stuck the flyer on my refrigerator so I wouldn't forget their wood-fired pizzas the next time I got hungry.

Now the Italian restaurant flyer gets lost in the shuffle of fridge wall craziness.

One month later, I drove back from the gym. My stomach growled, "Calories. Give me more calories!" And then I looked up. What did I see?

The billboard of my dreams. The billboard I had ignored and forgotten for a month. Yes, the Italian restaurant was calling my name.

In just a few minutes, I was seated in a booth, looking at the menu and texting my friends to join me for an Italian-calorie-overload.

Follow-up pays.

The Italian restaurant now has my repeat business and I am a walking salesman, recommending their food everywhere I go. The Italian restaurant has the repeat business of many of my friends.

We are committed, long-term customers. The Italian restaurant doesn't need to advertise to us again. We are fans.

How much did the Italian restaurant pay for the billboard? Probably thousands of dollars.

Did the Italian restaurant recoup the cost of the billboard? I think my friends and I paid for the billboard personally with our weekly consumption.

Now, if my friends and I ate enough food to pay for the billboard, just think about all the other drivers who saw that billboard. Did they have a similar experience? I bet some did. Between the billboard and some door hangers, the Italian restaurant kept following up with us and others. Yes, follow-up pays.

But what if the billboard was only up for one day? The Italian restaurant would have wasted its money.

Multiple exposures guarantee that when the timing is right for our prospects, we are right there, right in front of our prospects.

Billboards don't have feelings.

Every day the billboard announces that the Italian restaurant is open for business. Prospects see and ignore this billboard daily. Only a few prospects notice the billboard while driving their daily routine.

Does that mean prospects are rejecting the billboard every day? No. It just means that today is not their day. Maybe the timing will be better another day.

We need this type of attitude when following up with prospects. Our prospects forget about us. Our follow-up reminds our prospects of our offer. And who knows? Maybe today will be **their** day to take advantage of our offer.

Follow-up means we can serve that prospect when they are ready. This could mean a lifetime of repeat business.

The "mall sorting" effect.

The second effect of follow-up is the sorting effect. As prospects, we sort ourselves by ignoring all the offers that we don't need.

Our local mall has over 200 stores. I am not a frequent visitor. Personally, I spend as little time as possible at the mall.

But others? They love to shop. They live to shop. "Window shopping" isn't just a pastime. For them, "window shopping" is a career. These people constantly stroll the mall in the hopes of finding something new to buy.

Thousands of people go to the mall every week.

1. Some will go directly to one store and then leave. This is what I do.

2. Some people will go to a few stores and notice other stores during their mall visit.

3. And some, well, these professional "window shoppers" will go to every store.

Think of your follow-up like owning a store in the shopping mall. Your follow-up means you are visible to every person who walks past your store that day. If you are not there, these prospects will forget you exist.

These daily prospects sort themselves. You don't have to determine if their timing is right. Just think of yourself as one of the stores in the mall.

The cell phone store in the mall knows most of the shoppers are under a contract.

The jewelry store in the mall knows most of the shoppers don't need jewelry today.

The shoe store in the mall knows most of the shoppers bought shoes recently.

The burger stand in the mall food court knows most of the shoppers might want to eat something different today.

And in your business, for many of your prospects, today is simply not their day.

Rejection?

Thousands of people walk by each store in the mall every week. As a store owner, you don't even notice that the majority of mall shoppers walk past your store without even glancing at you. Your focus is only on those shoppers who walk into your store, because today is their day.

There isn't any rejection. Only sorting.

Just business as usual.

So if you are following up with multiple prospects, consider this as rejection-free as owning a store in the mall. Your job is to be in front of the prospect when the prospect's timing is right. That's it.

The "moving parade" effect.

Fear of rejection makes follow-up a problem. Our internal conversation might go like this:

"Oh, I might be bothering my prospect with a follow-up call. And now is not a good time to mail a reminder. What if I interrupt my prospect? I hope the prospect will just remember me, and remember me fondly. What if it isn't a good time for my prospect? What if my prospect says "No," and I am rejected? Shouldn't I just be looking for new prospects 100% of the time?"

Rejection has nothing to do with us personally. Rejection is usually not about our opportunity or product.

Rejection is usually only about the <u>timing</u> of the offer.

Most prospects are ideal for network marketing — provided that we present the opportunity when conditions are best for them. Your prospect is not ready or able to join your network marketing program 365 days a year.

For instance, for the first 18 years of the prospect's life, he is underage and unable to become a distributor. On his 18th birthday, does this prospect automatically become an entrepreneur?

Hardly. Maybe he becomes a race car driver, a professional party animal, a scholar, or something other than an ideal network marketing prospect.

Only sometime later will the prospect's conditions or situations be right to make a decision to join your network marketing program.

Think about yourself. When you joined your present network marketing program, the conditions were right for you. However, during the previous years, there were numerous times when the conditions were unfavorable for your entry into network marketing.

Maybe you had a personal relationship problem, a medical condition that demanded your entire attention, a job you loved, hobbies that held great interest, friendships you wanted to make, extensive travel plans or other ambitions that had your complete attention.

Then suddenly, the conditions were right for your entrance into network marketing. Maybe your job was no longer stable or became boring, perhaps you desired financial freedom, or possibly a career change just felt right. Maybe a certain network marketing product touched your family's life. For whatever reason, **the timing was right.**

So, we explain to our new distributor that his ten best friends **rejected the timing**, not the opportunity or the distributor personally. All ten friends will be excellent prospects at a later date when conditions change. (Of course, this assumes we didn't tell our friends they were stupid by refusing to join us today.)

The **moving parade** concept is another way to describe this to the new distributor. I would say something like this to the new distributor who is afraid of rejection:

"Imagine you are sitting on a grandstand watching a parade move by. The only prospects who would be qualified for your network marketing opportunity are those prospects who are marching **directly in front** of your grandstand. That means those same people are unqualified prospects **before** they pass your grandstand, and again become unqualified **after** they pass your grandstand.

"The only time the prospects are qualified is during the short period of time when they are marching directly in front of your grandstand.

"If they are not interested, **it has nothing to do with you.** It only means that the prospects are not marching directly in front of your grandstand at this time."

Now the sting and hurt of rejection goes away. Our distributor understands that the timing can make a huge difference in how our prospects respond.

Here is another way to look at how conditions affect the prospect.

Take a look at this prospect's day and notice the times when the prospect might be qualified for your network marketing opportunity.

6:00 a.m.: The alarm rings. John groans that he has to get out of bed. He wishes he had a business of his own where he could sleep late.

7:00 a.m.: John remembers that today is going to be one of his best days at work. Time for the yearly bonus checks.

8:00 a.m.: John's car is crushed by a speeding delivery truck. John remembers that he forgot to renew his auto insurance last week.

9:00 a.m.: John gets to the office and everyone is smiling. Maybe this will be a great day after all.

10:00 a.m.: The yearly bonus checks are distributed in sealed envelopes.

10:01 a.m.: Inside the envelopes are termination notices. The company has been purchased by a competitor and the employees are no longer needed.

10:30 a.m.: John gets a phone call from home that his wife has won the state lottery.

11:00 a.m.: The IRS tax collection team escorts John down to the local police station. Apparently there is a little discrepancy from last year's tax return.

And so, the day goes on.

If you invited John to an opportunity meeting at 6:00 a.m., he might be open to an alternate career. However, if you called John right after he learned that his wife won the state lottery, I am sure John would have other plans for the evening.

Several times throughout just one day, a prospect can turn from unqualified to qualified and back again. It's only a matter of **timing**, not a matter of personal rejection.

The story of Jay.

The three factors in follow-up are:

1. Repetition.

2. Sorting.

3. Moving parade.

Let's see them affect our prospect, Jay. Watch how Jay moves from ignoring the obvious to becoming a prospect in his story.

Jay is a born athlete, a natural football star through high school and college. But after college, Jay gets fat while sitting all day at his management job. Entertaining clients, fast food, and late nights at work pack on even more pounds and inches around his waistline.

Jay believes his washing machine shrinks his clothes, and constantly has to buy newer, bigger clothes.

Every day Jay sees weight-loss advertising on his social media pages, newspapers, billboards and television. He thinks, "I am in shape. I was a famous football player fifteen years ago."

One day Jay receives his 20-year high school reunion announcement in the mail. "Awesome! Time to see my old teammates!"

Totally in denial, Jay buys a bigger suit that fits. "Hmmm, I don't think I am that fat. The suits must be in metric sizes now."

At the reunion, a quick look at his old photos shows a much slimmer Jay. He thinks, "Oh, everyone puts on a couple of pounds in 20 years."

But when Jay meets his old girlfriend at the reunion, she blurts out …

"Oh Jay, you really got fat over the years!"

Now, Jay becomes a prospect for weight-loss products.

But which product? Should Jay pick a product from a random ad? Should he pick a product that he has seen on his social media pages?

No. Jay picks a product from a friend who kept in touch, who followed up with Jay even when Jay didn't think he was a prospect.

Because Jay's friend simply stayed in touch, and didn't pressure Jay to buy, there was trust and appreciation in their relationship.

Isn't that what we want our follow-up efforts to do? Of course. We want to be there with a solution when the time is right for the prospect.

So what is "follow-up" really?

Well, if timing is the issue in our prospect's life, then follow-up is just being there at the right time. This is a good reason to keep the relationship open and warm. When the time is right for the prospect, you want the prospect to think of you, and think of you fondly.

But what about the other reasons we need to follow up with our prospects? What happens when we have to follow up because we didn't give a very good presentation, or when our skills of communicating were less than adequate?

Moving closer to a decision.

In those cases, we should remember that the purpose of our follow-up should be to move the prospect **forward** toward a decision to join or buy.

Our reason for each contact with our prospect is to help the prospect feel better about us, and learn more about our business and what we offer.

The bottom line is that we want to move the prospect toward a "Yes" or "No" decision with every contact.

If we concentrate on providing more information and benefits to move our prospect forward, we will avoid idle chit-chat that wastes our prospect's time. Prospect respect that.

Compare these two scenarios:

1. You call the prospect and say,

"Oh, how are you doing? How is the weather where you are? What has been happening with your dog?"

We may be attempting to build rapport, but prospects are pressed for time. They have a job, family, television, Internet and more. Most prospects can't invest a lot of time in idle chit-chat.

2. Instead, you call your prospect and during your conversation say,

"I know you have to pay taxes on your wages, but did you know that having an extra part-time business could give you the same tax deductions that the big businesses get?"

Or, maybe you could say, "You mentioned earlier you had some interest in our magic vitamin product. I just found out two new things it can do. Would you like me to share those with you now?"

Or, maybe you could say, "When we met, you told me you love to travel. The company just announced a Hawaii trip incentive so we can qualify for a free trip. Would you like to go to Hawaii?"

So follow-up has two goals:

* Creating rapport and building a relationship.

* Moving the prospect forward toward a "Yes" or "No" decision.

Let's get started.

In the next chapters we will look at different ways to follow up with our prospects, and exactly what to say when we talk to them.

Create your movie.

Sometimes it is hard to find out exactly what our prospect is looking for. Some prospects look for:

* A guarantee that they will be successful.

* A product or service they believe has great value.

* A way to avoid talking to their friends.

* Something they can do online from home.

* A chance to do something exciting.

* A way to become super-rich.

* Something that is not overpriced.

* A mentor that understands their situation.

* No rejection.

If we don't know exactly what our prospects are looking for in an opportunity, then how can we serve them? We don't want to waste their time by presenting additional information that isn't relevant to their decision.

But, prospects seldom open up to us. There is an initial level of distrust in our first conversations. Prospects hold back from disclosing their wants and feelings. They fear that we will use high-pressure sales techniques to exploit their "hot buttons" for making a decision.

The "create your movie" technique.

This method will get your prospect to talk about his needs, wants, ambitions and what is important to him. It's easy.

In your conversation with the prospect, say this.

"It is easier to find exactly what you want, when you know exactly what it looks like. Imagine you are a big-time Hollywood producer. You have the power to create any movie you desire. If you created a movie of your perfect opportunity, what does that opportunity look like to you? What do you see?"

Sit back and let your prospect describe the perfect opportunity. Make a mental note of a few key points of their story.

* What did it cost to join?

* What did the prospect have to do?

* What steps did the prospect have to take?

* What did the bonus checks have to look like?

* Which activities were fun for the prospect?

And then ask the prospect, "How soon would you like that perfect opportunity to start happening in your life?"

Of course, the prospect answers, "Right now."

But there is a catch.

Your prospect described the "perfect" opportunity, and your opportunity doesn't even come close to the vision of your prospect. Probably no opportunity could come close to the perfect vision. So what do you say next? Try this.

"Wow. That would be awesome. A perfect opportunity in a perfect world. I guess you and I know that nothing in life is perfect, but hey, we can dream. The most important thing we can do in business is to **get into** business. While no opportunity is perfect, we can start building our business to get as close as possible. The difference is this. Dreamers just ... dream. Successful business people describe their dream, and then start working on making that dream happen. **When the time is right for you,** let's work together on making this business as close to your perfect dream as possible."

Notice that you didn't try to push for a close in this statement. You didn't lose rapport with your prospect for being too pushy. Instead, you accomplished these four things.

#1. You found out what the prospect is thinking, the criteria the prospect was using to make a decision to go forward.

#2. You politely let the prospect know that nothing is perfect. Not all the planets have to be in alignment before someone can take the first step forward.

#3. You mentioned that you and the prospect would be working together to make the prospect's dream closer to reality.

#4. You allowed the prospect some breathing room by saying "When the time is right for you ..." You allowed the prospect to feel in control of when he wants to get started. Of course, the obvious time to get started is immediately, but you didn't have to say that.

Communication is key.

Your chances of success improve when your prospect opens up and tells you what he is really thinking. This technique makes it easy for your prospect to talk.

You can use this technique whenever you are presenting or just prospecting and you will never lose rapport.

When they say "No" to what you offered.

"No" means … "No." That is why your prospect chose that word.

If we want to remain respectful, we must understand what they are saying "No" to. For example,

#1. They could be saying "No" to us.

They don't want to do business with us. We are not a good match for them. They want to work with someone else. Or maybe we offended them. In that case, future follow-up might be rude.

#2. They could be saying "No" to our opportunity or product.

They just aren't interested in what we have to offer. Maybe they have a prejudice against a certain product group or opportunity. Hey, if it isn't a fit for them, let's respect that and wish them well in their future searches.

For example, I don't wear white dress shirts. You sell white dress shirts. This is never going to work. You give me your best presentation. Your shirts have celebrity endorsements, and 10,000 five-star reviews on social media. The white dress shirts are featured on talk shows, they wash themselves, and they last forever.

100% of the time I will say "No" to your offer for white dress shirts.

Why? I just don't need or use that product.

However, two weeks later your company launches blue dress shirts. Awesome! Do you think I am interested now? There's only one way to find out: follow up with me.

So if your opportunity or product changes, you still have a reason to make a short follow-up contact with your prospects.

#3. They could be saying "No" to HOW we described our offer.

Think about it. Most prospects would love your products, your services, and more money. They are pre-sold.

However, they might not like how we described our offer. Simply changing a few words can make a huge difference in the results we experience. I bet you recognize the following example.

Imagine you are on a date. You say, "When I look in your eyes, time stands still." Or ... you could also say, "Your face would stop a clock!"

Now, both sentences describe the same thing. But one sentence will get a more favorable reaction, the other sentence might get you a slap in the face.

We can get a huge difference in results by changing how we describe and explain things.

So ask yourself, "Can I reposition my offer? Can I change how I describe my offer? Can I use different words?"

Here are some examples:

* "Our nutrition products will help you get fit." The prospect thinks that "fit" might involve exercise, and immediately turns down your offer. Instead, you could say, "Our nutrition products will turn your body into a fat-burning machine." And now the prospect is excited because he can visualize losing weight while using your products.

* "We can help you fire the boss." Sounds good to most prospects, but this prospect has his father-in-law as a boss. He doesn't want to lose the inheritance. Maybe we could have said, "Our business will give you an instant pay raise and you don't even have to ask the boss."

* "Join now and qualify for the free cruise of a lifetime." We didn't know that our prospect gets seasick. Instead, we could get a better response by saying, "Join now and start earning great part-time checks, so you can take those vacations you have been dreaming about."

* Instead of saying, "I will follow up with you weekly until you finally decide to join my business" ... maybe we could say, "Let's stay in touch. I know there is something we can do together in the future."

* "Join now and start making a list of 200 prospects you are afraid to call." Ouch. That is scary. We could say this as an alternative, "Let's just call your best friend first. Good friends love to do things together."

So check to see why your prospect is saying "No" to you. Many times they are only saying "No" to how the offer was described.

In that case, a simple change in your offer can turn that "No" into a brand-new distributor or customer.

"I need to think it over."

This is the most-feared objection for network marketers at the end of their presentation. So instead of thinking about ourselves and our agenda, let's first think about our prospects. They are thinking,

"I hate to make a decision."

Nobody likes to make decisions. Why do we have this fear?

We can all remember a bad decision from the past. The problem is, we remember that bad decision over and over again for years. That memory just makes us feel bad.

So the first reason prospects don't want to make a decision is because they don't want to feel bad if their decision does not work out.

The second reason your prospect hates to make a decision is ... humans hate change. Humans like what is comfortable to them. Change causes stress. Of course your prospect wants a change in his life, but he doesn't want to change personally to get there. This is just human nature.

Third, we have been trained by our job to not make decisions. If we are an employee, independent thoughts and decisions can sometimes get us fired.

Here is an example.

Imagine you are a clerk at a fast-food restaurant. A customer comes in and says, "I want to order a hamburger with ketchup on one side and only a pickle on the other side."

Now, what are you thinking?

"If I make this special hamburger for the customer, what will be the upside? I won't get a raise. There doesn't appear to be any incentive for me to do this for the customer. And if I do this for the customer, and the boss gets mad, I could get fired! There is no upside or incentive for me to do this, but there is a huge downside (getting fired) for doing this. I will tell the customer, 'I can't make a decision on this.'"

How your prospect tries to stay safe.

Because decisions mean bad things to your prospect, your prospect tries to avoid a decision by saying, "I need to think it over." And as long as the prospect is thinking it over, he feels he is safe.

But that's not true!

Not making a decision ... is a decision.

Whoops! When we don't make a decision to change, we are actually making a decision to stay with our current situation.

For example, if I stand in the middle of a busy highway, and a large truck is driving directly towards me, I could say to myself, "Hmmm, do I move to the left, or do I move to the right? I am afraid of making a decision, so I will stay right where I am right now."

Staying where I am, not moving out of the way of the oncoming truck, is a decision to be a victim of a soon-to-happen accident.

The bottom line is that everyone makes a decision every time. We either make a decision to change, or we make a decision to stay where we are.

Removing the "no decision" luxury from our prospect.

So our prospect says, "I need to think it over." What do we do next?

We remind the prospect that "thinking it over" is actually a decision to not take our offer, a decision to not change, a decision to keep his present circumstances.

How do we tell this to the prospect in a polite way that will maintain rapport and keep the doors open for further communication? Easy. We simply say:

"It is okay to make a decision to NOT join now and continue to work at that job you have no passion for. But it is also okay to make a decision to join now, and to start the countdown to an instant pay raise."

What have we done with those two sentences?

* We have made the prospect feel that it is okay to say, "No for now."

* There is no pressure from us. The prospect simply chooses to start changing now, or to continue with his present life as it is.

* We stayed in rapport. We didn't make the prospect feel bad if they didn't go with our agenda. We can continue to have a great conversation now and in the future.

* We showed the consequences of making the decision to delay or think it over.

* We showed the rewards of making a decision now.

Now, the prospect has to make a decision. He thinks, "Oh wow. I do have to make a decision. I can't pretend to put off the decision. Now, I have to make a choice."

And whichever choice the prospect makes, we are okay with that choice. It is the prospect's life, not our life. The prospect has to decide which path he wants to take.

All we do is offer an option.

Yes, we are giving the prospect a choice. That's it.

So there is no rejection to us or our opportunity. We shouldn't feel bad if our prospect's best option for his life is to not change.

Let's look at the formula for making these two sentences.

First sentence: "It is okay to make a decision to NOT join now and {insert the consequences of not changing}."

Second sentence: "However, it is also okay to make a decision to join now, and {insert benefits of our solution}."

Here are some of examples of this formula.

First sentence: "It is okay to make a decision to NOT join now and keep commuting to your job."

Second sentence: "However, it is also okay to make a decision to join now, and start building your at-home business and possibly in two years, just work out of your living room."

First sentence: "It is okay to make a decision to NOT start now and to continue sending the children to daycare."

Second sentence: "However, it is also okay to make a decision to start now, and if we work hard together, maybe next year you can be home with your children."

First sentence: "It is okay to make a decision to NOT start this evening and feel bad every morning when you go to work because you don't have a plan to escape the 9-to-5 job until you retire."

Second sentence: "However, it is also okay to make a decision to get started this evening, and feel good every morning because you know you are getting closer to having the time freedom you always wanted."

First sentence: "It is okay to make a decision to NOT start right away and to continue taking the family vacations at your mother-in-law's apartment."

Second sentence: "However, it is also okay to make a decision to get started this evening and build a part-time check, so that you can take those family vacations you told me you dreamed about."

First sentence: "It is okay to make a decision to NOT start this evening and continue to spend time searching for a plan to escape your job."

Second sentence: "However, it is also okay to make a decision to get started this evening, and start making your escape plan happen by building your business a little bit every day."

First sentence: "It is okay to make a decision to NOT start this evening and to continue hoping that the government will magically raise the retirement pensions."

Second sentence: "However, it is also okay to make a decision to get started this evening, and start building this part-time business so that in one year, we can possibly double your pension."

First sentence: "It is okay to make a decision to NOT start this evening and continue to wake up at 5:45 every morning to go to a job that you have no passion for."

Second sentence: "However, it is also okay to make a decision to get started this evening, and to start building this business, so that you can eventually sell your alarm clock to your neighbor."

What about retail sales?

If you were using these two sentences for a product or service, the formula would be:

First sentence: "It is okay to make a decision to NOT start using our product now and {insert the consequences of not changing}."

Second sentence: "However, it is also okay to make a decision to start using our product now, and {insert benefits of our solution}."

Remember, all we want to do is to let the prospect know he has choices, and that he is making a choice every time. Let's look at some product and service examples.

First sentence: "It is okay to make a decision to NOT begin our diet program now and to continue at the same weight, wishing something would change."

Second sentence: "However, it is also okay to make a decision to start our diet program now, so that in 30 days, you can be up to 12 pounds lighter with a lot more energy."

First sentence: "It is okay to make a decision to NOT start our magic night cream regimen now and to continue worrying about wrinkles every night before you go to sleep."

Second sentence: "However, it is also okay to make a decision to start our magic night cream regimen now so that you can see how much younger you will look in 30 days."

First sentence: "It is okay to make a decision to NOT change your utility supplier now and to keep paying the same higher rate."

Second sentence: "However, it is also okay to make a decision to have us supply the utilities you use, and allow us to send you a lower bill, so you can use that money to buy some gifts for the grandchildren."

First sentence: "It is okay to make a decision to NOT join our travel club tonight, and to continue paying a lot more than you should for your holidays."

Second sentence: "However, it is also okay to make a decision to join our travel club tonight, and to start getting five-star holidays for the price of an ordinary hotel room."

First sentence: "It is okay to make a decision to NOT use our natural cleaners that will preserve the environment and make your home safer for your grandchildren to visit."

Second sentence: "However, it is also okay to make a decision to start using our concentrated natural cleaners and to join us, and other families, in making our area a better place."

No imagination needed.

The key to these sentences is to be a good listener. You don't need a big imagination or need to be a mind-reader. All you have to do is listen to your prospect's needs and wants, and you will know exactly what to say to help your prospect make a decision.

This is fun, rejection-free, and there are never any bad feelings with your prospect.

Follow-up can be fun when we know what to say and what to do.

Listening for clues.

The purpose of a business is to solve problems. You probably remember that from my *Ice Breakers* book. If our prospects don't have problems, then there are no reasons for our businesses to exist.

So when we follow up, all we really have to do is find out which problem bothers them, and see if our opportunity, product or service can help them solve their problem. Sounds easy, doesn't it?

Find their problem, then solve it.

Here is where it all goes wrong. We try to solve their problem before we know what their problem is.

What does that look like in real life?

If we are giving our presentation, we are providing a solution. So giving the presentation is secondary. The first thing we have to do is find out what the problem is. And that can only be accomplished by listening.

Listening is a skill. And to listen deeply is an awesome skill for follow-up. When we listen beyond the words, we find the clues and the criteria that our prospects use to make their decisions.

The correct order is this.

43

#1. Listen.

#2. Solution.

Looks amazingly simple, but network marketers get so excited about their opportunity, products and services, they jump instantly to the solution and miss the clues they need to move their prospects forward.

Let's see how the clues appear in the following conversation. Your prospect responds to your follow-up call by saying:

"I still need to think things over. I just don't have any free time. My daughter takes up so much of my time with her school activities."

Now, when we hear this conversation at the surface level, it sounds like the prospect doesn't have any time.

But listen deeper. What clue is this prospect giving us? The prospect is telling us that her daughter is very important to her and deserves her time. She enjoys the time she spends with her daughter.

With this deeper understanding, our conversation can continue. We can move this prospect closer to joining our business by saying, "How would it feel for you to have a full-time income in this business, so you would have the time to attend every school activity?"

We are now talking about the real issues our prospect is experiencing in her mind. This deeper listening and communication creates deeper rapport and trust with our prospect, and serves our prospect better.

Let's practice listening now. Here are some follow-up conversations with prospects. Listen for the clues that indicate what they are really thinking. And then, follow up with this little phrase:

"How would it feel for you to ..."

The skeptic.

"I am not sure about the company. And I am not sure people would pay this much for your services. People are cheap and want the best deal."

This skeptic has issues with pricing. If you have great value for your services, you might say:

"How would it feel for you to know that we were voted #1 in value by our industry's trade magazine? They reported that our customers got the best overall price and service last year."

The busy executive.

"I don't want to play around with a small business. I need to focus on real money. My lifestyle demands an executive's salary."

The busy executive wants to write his own paycheck. He doesn't want to be told what he can earn. You might say this:

"How would it feel for you to have your own business, where you are the boss, and where you can finally write the paycheck you deserve?"

This is what the busy executive really wants to talk about.

The scared employee.

"I don't know anyone, and I have never been in business for myself before. I don't think this will work for me."

This scared employee wants the benefits of a part-time business, but is telling us that he doesn't have the confidence, that he can't do this alone. You might say this:

"How would it feel for you to have a full-time mentor and partner, someone working side-by-side with you until you are earning $1,000 extra a month?"

Yes, this is the conversation the scared employee would like to have with you.

What could you say next if the prospect is silent?

Sometimes we want to listen, but our prospect doesn't want to talk. The prospect is very "closed" and doesn't give us any clue what he is thinking.

Here are some examples of opening sentences that might help your prospect to feel comfortable and to start talking more:

* "Help me understand how a part-time income would change your life."

* "If you had an extra $500 a month, what would you spend it on?"

* "Where is the first place you would go on holiday if anywhere was possible?"

* "What is the most important reason you want to lose weight?"

These are all open-ended questions and statements that can't be answered with simple one-word answers. Getting your prospect to talk makes listening a lot easier.

Yes, listening makes it easy.

If you listen closely, your prospect will think you are a mind-reader. Your conversations will be better, your rapport will be better, and you can now move the prospect toward solving the real problem.

It is impossible to solve a problem unless we know what the problem is.

Listen first. Then, solve the problem.

Be incompetent at procrastinating.

Procrastination, like any habit, can be done badly. And you want to be terrible at procrastinating. So how do you mess up procrastinating?

With mini-habits.

Mini-habits destroy procrastination and fear. When you are facing a task you hate, simply apply mini-habits.

Here's how it works.

First, set the minimum effort it would take to do a task. In this case, if you were putting off making follow-up telephone calls, you set the minimum task to: "Making one follow-up telephone call."

That's it. That is the entire task.

Now, this task looks really small. It would be easier to do this one tiny task, "Making one follow-up telephone call," than to spend all the effort of worrying about and putting off your daily follow-up routine. Here is the choice in your mind:

1. Just make one follow-up call, or

2. Worry about the call, stress about rejection, and have this stress in the back of your mind all evening.

What will you do?

You will make the one little follow-up call and your task is completed for the day. That's it. It doesn't matter if no one answered your call, if you got voicemail, or if someone talked to you. All that matters is that you made that one little telephone call.

But, here is the secret.

Once you sit down and make the first telephone call, it is easy to make another call as long as you have your follow-up list in front of you. And then the momentum builds.

. Some days you make the one telephone follow-up call and quit. Other days, your momentum from the first call carries you into hours of follow-up conversations with your prospect list.

So make it easy on yourself. Just do the one mini-habit of only one follow-up telephone call.

The guilt and worry disappear. No more fears. No more feeling bad or dreading the experience.

Mini-habits rock, and can totally destroy procrastination.

Fear of the telephone is real.

It is easy for someone else to say, "Oh, don't be afraid of the telephone. It won't bite!"

Maybe the telephone won't bite, but the potential rejection from the follow-up telephone call is enough to paralyze us. We react to this fear with excuses such as:

* It is too early to call.

* It is too late to call.

* The prospect might be having dinner.

* The prospect could be tired after a long day at work.

Yes, our fear of the telephone continues. Our leader tries to help by telling us stories of heroes who failed. They say things such as, "Babe Ruth struck out 1,330 times (rejection) and hit 714 home runs (success) in his career. Isn't that an inspiring story?"

No, it is not an inspiring story. Babe Ruth felt bad 1,330 times. We don't want to feel bad! We want to avoid rejection.

How to guarantee rejection.

Many times we create rejection by asking direct questions that force our prospects into a corner. No one likes to be put on the defensive. Here are some questions and statements that will make prospects uncomfortable:

* "Well, have you finally made up your mind?"

* "I just called to see if you are now ready to start."

* "If you don't join today, you will miss the tsunami wave of momentum."

* "You have to join now so I can put 100 people in your group."

* "Whenever anybody hears about our products, they buy. Do you want to miss out on all that money?"

* "The industry has never seen a company like this one. We are projected to be #1. Don't be a loser and miss your chance."

These logical and emotional triggers don't work. These high-pressure sales techniques are from the door-to-door salesmen in the 1960s. They have no place in today's world. The prospects feel pressured by these statements and make the decision, "I will never answer this person's telephone call again. This is stressful, distasteful, and humiliating."

So the prospects tell us "No" in a variety of ways, just to get off the telephone call. They make up excuses and say:

* "It is not for me. I don't do these types of things."

* "I have to talk this over with my attorney, my spouse, my friends, and the squirrels in the back yard."

* "The timing isn't right for me. Doesn't look like a good time today, and tomorrow isn't looking very good either."

* "I just found out that a part-time business is against my employer's policies."

* "I don't have any time. I just bought the full release of my favorite soap opera."

* "I am afraid that if I earn any money, I will be in a higher tax bracket."

How to avoid rejection.
Technique #1: Give value.

When you give value, prospects look forward to your telephone call. They know you have their best interests at heart, and they will receive something valuable as a result. Your telephone conversations could go something like this:

"Hi John, Joe Distributor here. We talked briefly last week about my nutrition business, and I just got free tickets to this year's Natural Food Fest. Would it be okay if I mailed some tickets to you so that you and your family can enjoy the festival?"

"Hi John, Joe Distributor here. When we were at the opportunity meeting last week, you mentioned that saving money was important to you and your family. Well, the top tax accountant in the state is giving a free seminar on Friday. Thought you might like to attend. Here are the details ..."

"Hi John, Joe Distributor here. Last week when we talked, you had to leave quickly to pick up your daughters from school. Know you are busy, but wanted to know if you would like me to send you a copy of the new CD, *Creating Wealth While You Sleep*."

Are you closing your prospect on this telephone call? No. Are you creating rapport and keeping the lines of communication open? Yes. Your prospects won't dread your future telephone calls as they see you delivering value into their lives.

Sometimes it takes a while for the prospect to feel comfortable with you. Each impression or encounter moves the prospect closer to a better relationship with you and your opportunity.

Often you hear distributors moan, "Nobody returns my telephone calls. I leave a voicemail message, yet no one returns my calls."

· Well, the number one reason prospects don't return your telephone call is ... they don't want to talk to you!

They are afraid of some high-pressure sales pitch by a caller who is only concerned about himself. They don't want to spend time on the telephone with selfish, rude salespeople.

Providing value is one way to get prospects to return your telephone calls.

How to avoid rejection.
Technique #2: Update and ask a favor.

In Dale Carnegie's book, *How To Win Friends And Influence People*, he taught that one of the best ways to win over another person was to ask that person a favor.

It's magic.

So instead of just pushing our prospect for a decision, we can give our prospect a short, non-threatening update, and then ask a small favor. Want an example? Say:

"Hi John, Joe Distributor here. Our company just announced that this year's convention is going to be in Hawaii. You have relatives there, right? I just wanted to know if you could ask them about the best tourist places in Hawaii. I want to make sure my wife and I won't miss something really good."

Short update, and then a little favor. Easy.

And if John wants to go to Hawaii for free, John knows to ask you about how to qualify.

Now, the update you pass on to your prospect doesn't have to be brand-new news. Any news will do. Almost anything you announce about your business will be new to your prospect, so you should have plenty of ideas of what to say.

How to avoid rejection.
Technique #3: Agree and ask for a referral.

Part One: Say that it is okay not to act now.

Part Two: Ask for a referral.

Here is an example of this technique.

Example #1: "Hi John, Joe Distributor here. I know you don't have an interest in joining our business, but could you do me a favor? Our company just launched a free travel program, and I was wondering, do you know anyone who loves to travel a lot?"

Now, lots of things are happening in this example.

First, when you said, "I know you don't have an interest in joining our business," your prospect was relieved. Your prospect thought, "Oh, terrific! He is not going to pitch me! I feel better already."

Second, when you said,

"… but could you do me a favor?"

Your prospect thought, "Gee, you are such a nice person. You didn't try to sell me or force me to make a decision when you called. Of course, I would love to do a favor for you."

Your prospect feels good about your telephone call. And your prospect has three options:

#1. Give you a great referral of someone who loves to travel.

#2. Say, "Hey, I might be interested. I love to travel. Let's talk!" Hmmm, sometimes things change for your prospect, and now this business is a good fit.

#3. Say, "Thanks for calling, but no, I don't know anyone who loves to travel at the moment. I will let you know if I think of someone."

In all three options, the communication lines stay open. You haven't offended your prospect or caused the prospect to avoid future telephone calls.

Another example of this technique.

I like this example even more. All we have to do is change the first sentence from:

"I know you don't have an interest in joining our business, but could you do me a favor?"

To:

"I know the **timing wasn't right** when we last talked about my business, but could you do me a favor?"

In this second sentence, we **assume** that the prospect will join us in the future, when the prospect's timing is better. This makes it easier to re-open the conversation about our business opportunity, but still lets the prospect "off the hook" for now.

So now our conversation sounds like this:

"Hi John, Joe Distributor here. I know the **timing wasn't right** when we last talked about my business, but could you do me a favor? Our company just introduced a fast-start bonus, so a new distributor can earn $1,500 in their first 30 days. Do you know anyone who could use $1,500 in the next 30 days?"

And then sit back and let your prospect talk. Easy. And, non-threatening.

Or, maybe it would sound like this:

"Hi John, Joe Distributor here. I know the **timing wasn't right** when we last talked about our Quick-Slim-Body Kit, but could you do me a favor? Do you know anyone at your gym who is working out to lose weight?

This month the company is adding a free food planner in all the kits they ship."

The upside of rejection-free follow-up.

You followed up with your prospects. You didn't high-pressure your prospects or make them want to avoid your future telephone calls. In fact, your prospects enjoyed your telephone call.

You shared some news, asked for a small favor or referral, or gave your prospects more value in their lives. In doing this, you created a better, stronger bond with your prospects. Whether they decide to do business with you or not, you have still added to your biggest asset in life, your relationships with other people.

Relax, it's not about you.

You have a gold-plated vision board of all the things you want from your business. Your action plan is taped to your bathroom mirror. Your to-do list is updated daily. You can almost smell the impending success in your business.

Only one problem.

Fear.

Fear of the telephone, fear of talking to prospects, fear of rejection, and yes, fear of follow-up.

Why all this fear?

Because you are only thinking about yourself.

You worry if the prospect will like you, or if the prospect will say "No." You are completely focused on **your** feelings.

Think about your prospect.

It is easy to get rid of all these fears by simply focusing all your mental energy on serving your prospects. When you focus on your prospects, there is no room in your brain for worrying about yourself and your feelings.

Try this mental exercise before you follow up with prospects. Say this to yourself:

* "I want to answer my prospect's questions."

* "I want to help my prospect change his life."

* "I want to help my prospect feel confident about trying a new business."

* "I want to give my prospect confidence that I am here to help him get started."

* "I know my prospect wants change in his life. Let me share my opportunity so that he has options."

* "I want to let my prospect know that I care enough about him to follow up."

* "I want to let my prospect know that someone cares."

* "My obligation is to let my prospect know about my opportunity. The rest is up to the prospect."

Feel different?

This little exercise on focusing your thoughts entirely on your prospect leaves no room for fear in your mind. It's easy to do, and you will feel better almost immediately.

Your prospect will respond more favorably to your opportunity because the prospect feels your concern and interest in them.

So, instead of chanting affirmations, staring at your vision board, and thinking about all the stuff you want, simply make your whole conversation about the prospect.

Just think of your follow-up as a service to the prospect. Think, "Hey, my obligation is simply to inform the prospect and help the prospect. It is up to the prospect to make a decision if now is the time to improve his life, or not."

By removing yourself from your thoughts, and placing your thoughts on the prospect, fear and procrastination naturally go away.

Need some easy words to say to reinforce this focus?

Try these phrases:

* "This may or may not be for you."

* "Timing is personal. It is up to you to decide when you want to move forward."

* "Here is what we do. See if it is a fit for you."

* "What would you like to know first?"

* "What would you like to know next?"

* "Would you like to hear how others handled that problem?"

* "We either make a decision to move forward, or we make a decision to stay where we are. Only **you** know what is right for you."

Not only do these phrases make you feel comfortable, they also make the prospect understand that you care about him.

Now your follow-up conversations can feel better.

Be the expert.

Feel uncomfortable talking with prospects? Feel a bit intimidated when prospects ask questions or make objections? Our self-talk sometimes deteriorates into questions such as:

* What will they really think of me?

* What if I goof up?

* What if I forget some details?

* What if I give them the wrong info on the products?

* What if the compensation plan presentation isn't perfect?

We all want more self-confidence, but fear is a powerful emotion. So how do we overcome our fears of talking to prospects?

By becoming the expert in our business.

We feel more confident when we know more than our prospects. Want an example?

Imagine that tomorrow you are asked to talk to 100 medical graduate students about brain surgery. The problem is that you know nothing about brain surgery. Feeling a bit anxious?

You surf the Internet to pick up some medical jargon and big words. You try to memorize some important facts, but it is overwhelming. You are thinking, "What if they ask me a question? What if they realize I know nothing? What if they start complaining during my talk?"

You know the medical students know more than you do. This is going to be ugly. You dread the thought of beginning your talk. You start thinking of excuses to avoid your talk.

Sound familiar?

But also imagine this scenario.

Your child is in first grade. Your child's teacher asks you to come in and do a talk on how to tie your shoes. Now, this is going to be easier. No need for you to memorize anything. You have tied your shoes thousands of times. You won't even need a PowerPoint presentation. You can do this talk without notes.

How do you feel? More confident? You are not worried that the first-graders will ask tough questions. You are ready right now.

The next day you arrive at the classroom. The students are excited. Here's someone new to talk to them. This is going to be great.

If the students have a question, you are ready. They sense your self-confidence. You are a star!

The students practice. They have fun.

And you? You never once worried or cared about what the students thought of you. You were just focused on giving them value.

Ah, life is good when you are the expert.

So what about your business?

You know more about your business than most of your prospects. In their eyes, you are the expert. They haven't been to your company's training, and they certainly don't know about your products and compensation plan. You know more than they do.

So carry that confidence with you when you talk to prospects.

Want to be even more confident? Well, that is easy. Just learn more skills in your business, and your prospects will sense your competency.

No prospect wants to follow someone who is incompetent, who doesn't know where he is going, and doesn't have the skills to get there.

So the more skills you learn, the easier it will be to talk to prospects, and to enroll prospects into your business.

Verbal conflict.

There is an old saying, "You can win the battle, but lose the war."

Sure, you can use words to corner your prospect, to trap your prospect, and even use your prospect's words against him. Yes, you can be right. You can win.

And your prospect will never answer your telephone calls again.

To make follow-up civil and enjoyable to all, we don't want to become a high-pressure closing machine.Why? Because even if you close your prospect against his will, this is an all-volunteer business. Your prospect will quit at the first opportunity.

Closing takes on a new meaning in network marketing.

This is not a one-time sale. This could be a relationship that lasts a lifetime. A quick, high-pressure close isn't appropriate.

You want your prospect to want your opportunity. You want your prospect to be excited to get started. This won't happen if you push, shove, embarrass and force your prospect to join.

What is verbal conflict?

Think of the difference between a friendly conversation, and a battle of wits. In a battle of wits, your prospect isn't even listening to you. While you are talking, the prospect is thinking about what to say to support his position. No listening. It could get ugly.

Trapping the prospect or manipulating what the prospect says is anti-social. Now, that's not good for a business that requires relationships.

Here are some phrases that may set off a verbal conflict. Now, there may be places in your business for some of these phrases, but consider how the prospect would feel if you used these phrases on a follow-up telephone call, early in your relationship.

* "So, you want to get started now or continue to procrastinate?"

* "I only have time for serious players. Are you serious?"

* "So what is it going to take to get you to make a decision today?"

* "Now, you promise you will watch the video, right? You are a person who keeps their commitments, aren't you?"

* "Winners win. Losers procrastinate. So what's it going to be?"

* "Are you in, or are you out?"

* "If I could show you how to start earning that income now, would you be ready to commit today?"

* "You told me you wanted a business. Now you are hesitating. Is there something I missed?"

All of these statements or questions could irritate or be misinterpreted by our prospect. Why take the risk?

What is the opposite of verbal conflict?

Instead of participating in verbal conflict, try focusing on what you and your prospect have in common. You create rapport with agreement, not with conflict.

So what do you and your prospect have in common? Talk about what you agree upon instead. Some examples:

* "Well, we all hate how jobs take up so much of our time."

* "Everyone wants changes to improve their lives."

* "It certainly is hard to get by on one paycheck."

* "No one knows how to do a business before they start."

* "Sometimes the first step is the hardest."

* "Control of our time is important."

* "Life doesn't last forever."

* "There will never be a perfect time to start."

* "I felt the same way when I first saw this."

* "Most people have the same concerns."

Network marketing is a relationship business, not a one-time transaction. Relationships can take time. Verbal conflict during an initial follow-up can delay or even ruin that relationship.

Focus on what you agree upon now, and that will be your foundation to build your relationship.

How to improve your posture with your prospects.

Prospects can smell desperation. Ouch!

When we have a limited number of prospects, we get stressed. If we have only one prospect, we think, "Oh no, don't offend this prospect or I won't have any prospects and I'm finished!" So we simply visit and chit-chat, never asking for a commitment.

Prospects sense our poor posture and they lose confidence in us. You see, prospects are looking for:

1. Someone to follow.

2. Someone who knows where they are going.

3. Someone who has the skills to get there.

Prospects don't like where they are. That is why they are interested in our opportunity.

So how do you give prospects confidence in you? How do you have a confident posture?

By having more prospects.

When you are busy, with too many people to talk to, you are not attached to the decision of any particular prospect.

You are too busy deciding which of your prospects are ready now. Now each prospect feels the need to qualify to get your attention. Prospects now reach out to you, wanting to attach themselves to your momentum.

You are not asking, begging, or pleading for prospects to join. Instead, you simply show the prospects that you are going somewhere, and they can join with you or be left behind.

This changes the conversation. Prospects want to be with someone who is going places. They start asking you "buying questions" such as:

* What was that product called again?

* How much were the different packages?

* What is my monthly commitment?

* How can I break even or earn my first check?

* How can I make $500 this month?

* When is the next meeting?

* Do you think you can help me get started?

* I would like to know more about ...

More prospects.

This is the simplest, surest way to a better posture. So if you feel shy, or a bit intimidated by prospects, immediately get more prospects to contact. Now you won't worry if a single prospect decides not to join or buy. You have plenty of other prospects to talk to.

Yes, prospects can smell desperation.

Don't be desperate.

You are not the center of the universe.

Time to follow up with that important prospect. In the last conversation, you told your prospect:

1. You have the best pay plan.

2. You have the best product.

3. You have the best testimonials ever.

And now, your prospect admits forgetting all that important stuff you told him. Plus, your prospect did not go to your website, listen to the testimonials, or watch the company video!

First rule of rapport: Let it slide.

Don't embarrass the prospect by saying things such as:

* "You promised you were going to watch it."

* "Don't you understand how important the timing is?"

* "I only have time for serious people."

* "Did you remember the superstar bonus I presented?"

* "You're going to miss the boat!"

* "I can't believe you just don't get it."

Hey, this prospect isn't someone that you sell to one time, and then never see again. Hopefully, this will be a long-term relationship. All of the previous statements activate the salesman alarm. Sure, a high-pressure close might work for today, but tomorrow this prospect won't return your telephone calls.

What should I say when this happens?

"I understand."

Yes, this is a complete sentence. When you say that you understand, you have agreed with your prospect. People like people who agree with them. If there is agreement, there is open communication. Disagreement closes minds.

Agreement tells the prospect that you are on his side, and that you respect his views. You are not trying to force the prospect to think like you.

You have probably heard the old saying that we have two ears and one mouth, so we should listen twice as much as we speak. This short two-word sentence, "I understand," will immediately allow the prospect the opportunity to start talking about what he is thinking.

Remember, we are problem-solvers. Let the prospect talk so we know which problems we will need to solve.

What do you say next if the prospect is silent?

Since the prospect has forgotten us, and everything we told him, we can re-open the conversation by asking this simple question.

"What would you like to know first?"

At this time the prospect will reveal if he is truly interested now, or if now is simply not "his time" to join. The prospect will give you a "stop sign" or a "buy sign," so listen closely.

What is a "stop sign" statement?

It is impolite to say "No" directly to someone, so your prospect will use a "stop sign" statement such as:

* I am not interested.

* I don't have time.

* Please stop calling me.

* No, thank you.

Take a hint. The prospect is saying "No for now" and that's okay. Maybe you didn't have strong rapport, or maybe the prospect is facing personal challenges.

But if today is not your prospect's day, don't close the door on the prospect's future. Maybe in a month, or in several months, things could change.

Wes Linden, author of *79 Network Marketing Tips For Fast-Track Success*, keeps almost everyone in rapport by saying,

"I understand. That's no problem. Timing is the most important thing. Would it be okay if I keep in touch from time to time? To find out how you are doing and to let you know how we are doing?"

Pretty awesome. No one says "No" to Wes with this polite reply. Everyone says, "Yes, of course."

Then Wes puts their contact information into his spiral-bound notebook that he calls, "No For Now." Every day that notebook fills with more and more prospects that Wes can follow up with later, and his prospects gave him permission to do it!

This gives you a chance to re-visit at a better time in the prospect's life.

Wes has a notebook for every year he is in the business. When Wes needs someone to talk to, he literally has hundreds and hundreds of people he can call.

When I passed on this great idea from Wes, a workshop attendee said that he was going to call his own follow-up notebook, "Yes For Later." Now, that is a positive spin on this idea!

Wes Linden's philosophy is:

"Our job isn't to close people, it is to open them."

What is a "buy sign" statement?

After starting the conversation with, "What would you like to know first?" the prospect says:

* Do people really desire this product?

* Tell me again how the pay plan works.

* How many hours a week do you think this will take?

* Will I have to know a lot of people?

* So how soon do you think I could be earning an extra $300 a month?

* Is there training?

Now your prospect is looking for reasons to join, instead of reasons not to join. Your conversation will be effortless as you simply answer your prospect's questions as best you can. Your prospect is comfortable as you are allowing the prospect to control the direction and flow of information.

The worst thing we can do is do all of the talking. Prospects want to buy. They don't like to be sold.

What if I don't know the answer?

This works in your favor. Prospects don't expect you to be a walking Wikipedia. If you don't know, the prospect realizes that he doesn't have to be an expert to be successful. Most tough questions can be answered by saying, "That is a great question to ask when you attend your first company training."

One of the biggest reasons prospects don't join is that they can't see themselves doing the business. Keep it simple. Decisions are easier when the choices are simple.

The proposal.

During his lunch break in the local park, a young single man says to himself, "Today is a good day to find a wife!"

So he walks up to the first woman he sees and asks, "Will you marry me?"

A shocked look crosses the woman's face as she rushes around him and quickly runs away.

The young man thinks, "Maybe I asked my question too quietly and she didn't understand."

So to the next woman who walks by, he shouts, "WILL YOU MARRY ME?"

Odd. She too runs away without answering his question. What could be wrong?

Confused, he looks at his clothes. Hmm, well-dressed. Checks his breath, and everything smells okay. And he even has his work badge still clipped to his belt so it's obvious he has a job.

After a few more failures, the young man returns to work.

He wonders why every woman said "No" or simply hurried away.

And then the reason becomes clear in his mind. Yes, his prospects just need a chance to build rapport so there is trust and belief. People won't do business with people they don't trust and believe.

It turns out it is hard to build trust and belief if you are shouting at women passing by your park bench. Not the ideal way to create that long-term relationship.

A normal courting relationship might have the following events:

* Initial meeting.

* Initial date.

* Repeat date.

* Long telephone conversations.

* Meeting someone's friends.

* Meeting the family.

* Talking about future plans, etc.

And after all that follow-up to the initial meeting, then the original question, "Will you marry me?" has a better chance of success.

Will you join me in my business?

How about our prospects? Won't they feel more comfortable after multiple contacts and chances to build some sort of relationship and trust? Of course.

Because we don't have a solid rapport with some prospects, they won't immediately make the commitment to join. And the more hype and benefits we throw at them on the initial contact, well, the faster they want to run away.

We can't start by saying:

* "Our product will let you lose 50 pounds in a week."

* "Our service is the best and all our competitors are crooks."

* "You can retire from your job in only seven hours."

* "Only losers turn this great deal down."

* "Don't let your negative loser friends at work talk you out of this."

* "Every movie star is already in our business under a secret name."

* "Act now. If you wait until tomorrow, it's too late."

* "Commit now to change your life. You don't have any time to think this over."

* "We are the best. Do you have trouble making good decisions?"

* "Any three-year-old can see this is a good opportunity. Do you have a problem with that?"

* "Don't you love your family?"

* "Become a millionaire overnight while you sleep."

* "Why are you making a decision to delay and keep supporting your boss' lifestyle?"

* "Do you have something against earning money?"

If rapport isn't there, asking prospects to make a major life choice is unfair. This could be a big commitment for them, so they want to feel comfortable with us.

And maybe our prospect doesn't even want to "marry our business." Instead, the prospect might simply want to join to use our product, to participate in the self-development, or to enjoy the social life with more positive friends. Not everyone will have the same agenda.

So instead of going too fast, or asking for too much commitment, we could talk about smaller commitments along the way. For example:

* To come to an opportunity meeting to meet other people who are involved.

* To try one product to see personal results.

* To listen to an informative audio on how our product works.

* To have a three-way call with a successful leader who could share his story and insights.

* To keep an open mind and to have another conversation in 30 days to see if anything has changed in the prospect's life.

* To look at some testimonials of people earning $500 a month.

The first follow-up doesn't have to be, "Make a major life choice now." We have time. The prospect has time.

And maybe the prospect only wants to "date" for a while to see how things go. Maybe he'd like a chance to get to know you better.

As a professional network marketer, we should be sensitive to go at the speed the prospect desires. Now, that doesn't mean slow. With better rapport skills, we can create that relationship much faster. But we always want to go at a pace that is comfortable for our prospect.

Automatic follow-up.

Are you uncomfortable and shy on the telephone? Do you hate calling someone over and over again asking, "Uh, have you read the information I sent you? Have you made a decision? Have your circumstances changed?"

Using automatic follow-up relieves you of the wasted time you invest in leaving messages that no one returns. And if you wonder why prospects don't return your telephone calls, here is why.

They don't want to talk to you.

Maybe they are afraid to say "No" ... or maybe it isn't the right time. But remember, the reason prospects don't call you back is because they don't want to say "Yes" to what you offered earlier.

Can that change? Sure.

But for now, their answer is "No."

So how does automatic follow-up work?

Automatic follow-up consistently reminds the prospect of the offer you have made. Every day, or every week, they remember your offer. When it is their time to take advantage of your offer, they will remember you. And,

81

they'll remember you fondly because you didn't harass them with constant telephone calls.

Automatic follow-up means:

1. No more telephone calls, voicemail, or chances of rejection.

2. Your follow-up time is reduced to zero so you can invest that time in more prospecting.

The technique you will use to automatically follow up is a time-delayed word picture. If you have not learned the skill of creating word pictures yet, here is a short explanation.

A word picture is using words in a special way to create a story. Your prospect sees the story in his mind. It's like telling a story and having your prospect see the story come to life in a movie inside of his head.

Word pictures automatically help with procrastination, **but by adding an event to the story,** your prospect is reminded of the story every time the event happens.

When you create a good word picture, your prospects can't get it out of their minds.

Here is an example:

Imagine that you are talking to a prospect. At the end of your presentation he says:

"I need to think it over. I have to talk it over with my dog and my lawyer. I will get back to you in a couple of months."

Say to your prospect:

"Hey! I am glad you want to think it over. Could you do me a favor?

"Tomorrow morning when you wake up to go to work, and you get into your car at 7 a.m., pull your car keys out of your pocket. Just before you put them in the ignition, do me a favor. Would you just ask yourself this question?

"'Do I really want to be getting up and leaving my family at 7 a.m. and commuting to work and fighting all that traffic? And is this the car of my dreams?'

"That's all – could you just ask yourself that?"

The prospect will say:

"Sure, no problem."

What happens the next morning?

The time-delayed effect of word pictures kicks in.

The next morning your prospect wakes up, goes out to his car, pulls his keys out of his pocket, puts them into the ignition, and what is he going to think?

Your prospect will think,

"Wow, do I really want to be getting up at 7 a.m., leaving my family and commuting all the way to work? And is this 1973 Pinto really the car of my dreams? Maybe I should rethink that opportunity that they talked about last night."

But, here is the magic. What will happen the morning after that? The same thoughts will go through your prospect's mind.

And the next morning.

And the next morning.

Your prospect will always be thinking of you and your opportunity. And when the timing is right, such as when his boss yells at him or there is a big traffic jam, you will be in the forefront of his mind. Your prospect will be calling you to tell you that now is the time for him to take action.

Do you want another example?

You finish your presentation to a young lady and she says:

"Oh, I need to think it over. I need to talk to my lawyer, my cat, my astrologer and my psychic."

You would then say this:

"Could you do me a favor? Next time you get your paycheck, could you do this? When you rip open that paycheck envelope, pull out your paycheck, hold it up to the light and rub it between your thumb and forefinger and ask yourself this question: 'Is that all that I am worth?'"

Well, what is going to happen the next time that she gets her paycheck?

She will rip open the paycheck envelope. But, she probably won't hold the paycheck up to the light. Someone might see her and think that she is strange.

But she will think to herself:

"Is that all that I'm worth?

"You know what? I had to work overtime three days last week. And the person next to me never showers. That other person talks too much. I am tired of fighting traffic. They don't appreciate me. They don't give me a raise. I missed my daughter's violin concert last week by working overtime. And I hate these stupid reports. Maybe I should take a look at something else. Maybe I should take advantage of that opportunity I saw last month."

And that's the time-delayed effect of using word pictures to automatically follow up with your prospects.

"I will start my diet ... next week."

You finish your presentation on your wonderful diet products. Even though you convinced your prospect that your Wonderful Diet Program will take off the weight, and keep the weight off forever, your prospect hesitates.

Why? Maybe your prospect is still thinking this inside of his head:

"I like my favorite foods. Plus, eating out with others is my favorite social pastime. It is impossible for me to go to bed with an empty stomach. I don't like feeling hungry. I tried fasting once, but I got hungry 30 minutes later. Maybe I will start dieting seriously next week ... or the week after."

So how will you remind your prospect that your diet program is right for him? Calling your prospect every week and asking, "Are you still fat?" might be a recipe for rejection. Instead, you could give your prospect this time-delayed word picture:

"It is okay to make a decision to not start your diet today. I understand. But, could you do me a favor?

"Each morning when you put on your pants and buckle your belt, could you ask yourself this little question? 'Is today the day I change my life and start the Wonderful Diet Program?'"

So guess what happens? Every day when your prospect gets dressed, he briefly thinks about you and the Wonderful Diet Program. And when the time is right for the prospect to make a change in his life, well, your words have almost become a daily friend. Your prospect is calling you to start his diet.

"Your night cream sounds good, but not now."

Your prospect loves the idea of using the Wonderful Night Cream to make her skin younger while she sleeps. But your Wonderful Night Cream is a bit expensive, and she has six months of night cream sitting on her shelf at home. Of course she hesitates and says, "Your night cream sounds good, but not now. Let me use up my old night cream and then get back to you if I am interested."

You reply, "No problem. I understand you want to use up your six months' supply of your old night cream. I felt the same way when I was introduced to the Wonderful Night Cream. But I had a problem. Every morning when I woke up and looked into the mirror, I asked myself, 'Do I want to wake up every morning with these bags under my eyes? Or do I want to start using the Wonderful Night Cream now?'"

Guess what your prospect is going to think that evening when her head touches the pillow?

Yes, you will be reminding her every night of your Wonderful Night Cream.

Automatic follow-up is not the only way to follow up with your prospects, but it does save time. It is perfect for shy distributors who feel uncomfortable with telephone calls to prospects who are not ready to take action yet.

Personal follow-up, with no rejection.

Why do we feel guilty calling our prospects to see if today is their time to make a decision?

Maybe we are interrupting their day. Or, maybe we fear they have decided to say "No," and we don't want to hear that.

It is so easy to find reasons not to follow up.

So let's start with the easiest and safest way to follow up with our prospects, by email. While this is a low-touch follow-up technique, it is rejection-free and very safe for shy people.

First, let's remind ourselves of the downside to email. Many people may not open your email. Or worse, your email is delivered to their spam folder, never to be seen.

Why would your uninterested prospect want to open your email?

The secret is to provide **value** with each email. This will train your prospect to open every email from you, because he or she expects to receive value.

What kind of value can you include in your email?

* An article that talks about a solution to your prospect's problem.

* A link to important information your prospect would like to know. For example, that 90% of workers don't have enough money for retirement.

* A testimonial about how a customer has used your product or opportunity. Real stories about real people are always interesting.

* A simple resource that would enhance your prospect's life. This resource doesn't have to be associated with your product or opportunity. Just something that is helpful.

* Or, even an appropriate joke that your prospect could share with his or her friends. Most people love a good joke, and love to tell a new joke to their friends.

If you don't add value with each email, you will train your prospect to quickly delete your emails as nothing more than a sales pitch to buy or join. Providing value is the key.

Need more reasons to send a
follow-up email to your prospect?

* Announce an upcoming price increase in your product, service, or enrollment fee to join your opportunity. This is a courteous reminder to let your prospect know about his chance to save.

* Maybe a product has a limited supply. That supply may be decreasing quickly and this may be the last chance for your prospect to buy.

* Let him know about an upcoming sale or discount of your product or service.

* Inform him that the current sales price of your product or service is ending soon.

* Offer a free trial of your product or service.

* Offer an enhanced or upgraded version of your product or service for the same basic price.

* Educate your prospect on a new way to use your product or service.

* Offer a bonus if your prospect purchases now.

* Include a link to a recent article that talks about your product, service, or opportunity.

* Send a link to a video that talks about your product, service or opportunity.

Yes, there are lots of reasons to keep in contact with your prospect. Your competition won't have the discipline to keep in touch, so you will stand out with your prospect.

Are you in the business for the long haul?

A personal newsletter can keep your warm market interested in you and your business.

Here is the technique:

Once a month, write a short newsletter with some updates in your life. This newsletter will go to your family, friends, coworkers and even your cold prospects. People enjoy taking a little peek inside another person's life.

Remember those once-a-year letters you get from friends at Christmas that update you on what happened to them over the past year? Well, maybe your newsletter shouldn't be that long and boring. I am sure you can do a more interesting version.

Talk about yourself and your personal experiences during the month. People like to know about a job change, a relationship change, or maybe that you purchased a new car. You can even talk about your dog or cat.

But somewhere in your newsletter, mention your network marketing business. You could tell the story about the customer who called you with a great testimonial and thanked you for your product. Or, describe the conversation you had with a distributor about how much fun you had at a big company event. This is not the time to use hard-core sales benefits and calls to action. Instead, you just want to let them know that you are still doing "that thing." They will be impressed with your persistency.

We know that prospects are looking for changes in their life.

* They are desperate for someone to follow.

* They want to follow someone who knows where he or she is going.

* And they want to follow someone who knows how to get there.

Yes, they are checking to see if you have the skills for your business. Nobody wants to follow someone who is unsure and constantly changes direction.

When you show a stable track record, even your worst skeptics will be impressed with your long-term commitment. Yes, network marketing gets easier over time. You build your credibility with your consistency.

When the readers of your personal newsletter have events in their lives that make them want to change careers, they will think of you, and think of you fondly. They will feel safe joining with you, because they have seen your long-term commitment.

Your personal newsletter does not have to be very long. You just want it to be a little update on what happened to you that month. In time, people will look forward to your newsletter. So make sure to train them to open your email by avoiding direct sales pitches in your newsletter.

Be unique.

Twenty five years ago, mail-order marketing was at its peak. Every major company had a catalog. We received catalogs monthly, quarterly, holiday versions and special limited-time offers. Instead of going to the mall, we could shop at home at our leisure while watching television.

We browsed the catalogs, called a toll-free telephone number, and products magically arrived on our doorstep. Business at the post office was booming because every company wanted to send out a catalog.

Fast forward a few years, and the term "junk mail" became very real. Yes, we received too much mail and it all looked the same. Most people would sort through their junk mail over the trash can. If it didn't look interesting within a second it went in the trash. Maybe that is how we were trained to delete junk email so quickly.

Yet some companies survived the junk mail crash of 1999. Even today, companies still use catalogs in addition to all the email lists, websites, social media, etc.

How did they survive?

They were **unique**.

They consistently delivered their value to us in a slightly different way to stand out from the crowd.

* Instead of a boring white envelope, they used a blue envelope.

* Instead of impersonal computerized address labels, they wrote the address by hand.

* Instead of marketing buzzwords, their messages felt more personal.

The best way to avoid being trashed as junk mail is to not look like junk mail.

Today, it's even worse. Email is inexpensive to send, so now we are flooded with junk emails and offers. It is obvious which messages are spam just by reading the subject lines of the emails. After a few hundred mind-numbing, overhyped subject lines, it is easy to identify email that is junk, and email from friends.

Not familiar with mind-numbing, overhyped subject lines? Here are a few to start with:

"Make $1,000,000 in the next 30 days!"

"We are #1!"

"We build your downline for you. No work!"

"Basement opportunity. Better than a ground-floor opportunity."

"Industry experts are predicting this one…"

"Join now before it is too late."

Emails with these subject lines will be quickly deleted. Our follow-up strategy will have to be more unique and interesting.

For example, if our competition is using emails, we might stand out by sending a physical postcard. We have to get our follow-up communications noticed.

If our competition is flooding social media, what could we do that is different?

* Could we offer some sort of interactivity such as getting them to vote on a survey?

* Do we have something special that people want to share?

* Are we viewed as a real person or just another salesman?

* Could we have an engaging short video?

Prospects are in a trance.

Information overload. Advertising overload. Endless emails and social media. It's a blur to our prospects. After a while, it all looks the same.

With a little effort, we can stand out from the crowd and our follow-up can get noticed. After all, what good is our follow-up campaign if no one sees it?

While everyone is flooding the Internet, or using the telephone to follow up, the next chapter shows one way you can be different.

With postcards.

Postcards ... they have to be noticed.

Yes, using the mail is "old school," but that is what makes postcards stand out and gets prospects to notice your message.

The mail service is here to stay for a long time. Why? So people can get their bills and advertisers can reach more people. Yes, online is the future, but not everyone is ready to change yet.

Mail makes people feel special. Think about this.

Do you normally get an invitation to attend someone's wedding by email? Or do you receive a nicely-designed, printed invitation?

For special occasions, a mailed invitation tells people they are special.

Deleting an email? Easy. But if someone takes the time to mail you something, it must be important.

Now, you might be thinking, "Mail a follow-up communication? That will take more time. That will cost a bit of money."

Yes, it will. But isn't a great prospect worth your time and a bit of money? If you stand out from the crowd and show that you care, this prospect could earn you thousands of dollars a month for the rest of your life. A very personal communication will impress your prospect.

Remember, people are really joining **you**. They are looking for that guide who knows where he or she is going, and knows how to get there.

So how do you effectively use the mail to get people to join you?

Enter the postcard solution.

Postcards are inexpensive to buy and inexpensive to mail. Plus, the best part is ... postcards mean that you are totally safe from any rejection. You never have to hear someone say, "No!" over the telephone.

Using postcards to motivate prospects to join you is simple. Remember, if you took the time to send a postcard, they know you are thinking about them, and prospects love to feel important.

Just the idea that you ask prospects for a mailing address also makes them feel special. They will be wondering what you are going to send them in the mail. Curiosity is on your side.

And finally, a postcard shows that you remembered them as a **person**, not just a phone number or a name on your email follow-up list.

A picture is worth a thousand words.

Postcards can also have pictures which spark an emotional response. People love looking at pictures. No one likes throwing pictures away. If your prospects keep your postcards, those images and messages will continue to be in their minds.

So what kind of postcards can you send?

#1. It's on sale!

Do you have a product promotion you could announce? Buy one product, get another product free? Or maybe you could offer a special trial size of your product or a free trial of your service?

#2. I am at the convention.

Show a picture of you with hundreds or thousands of fellow attendees. Social proof, that others are involved, removes one of the obstacles that your prospects might have. When your prospects see all those other happy people involved, they feel more comfortable about giving your business a try.

#3. I am on vacation.

The next time you are on vacation, send your prospects a postcard. Whether your bonus check paid for the entire vacation, or a few nights in the hotel, your prospects will see that your business can lead to fun vacations. They can picture themselves enjoying a vacation with their families.

#4. A local attraction.

Use a picture of a local attraction with a quick message from you that says, "I liked this attraction and it reminded me to get back in contact with you. Hope you are doing well."

No sales pitch. Just a reminder that you remember the prospect as a real person, not just a name on a list.

#5. Promote your product or service.

Create your own postcard. Take fun pictures with your products or services and get them printed. If you want to do just a few postcards, simply search for "peel and stick postcards" or go to your local office supply store. You can take photos and turn them into real postcards in seconds. People will have a hard time throwing them away because it has your picture on it.

What kind of message should you put on the postcard?

Make sure your offer is not a time-sensitive offer. Remember, delivery depends on the post office, so it could take several days to have your postcard delivered.

Your postcard is designed to build a trusted relationship with your prospect. So your message doesn't have to be a full-blown opportunity presentation, just a reason to stay in contact. Here are some sample short messages.

* "We are enjoying our tax-deductible holiday here at the company convention. I always wanted to see new cities, and the family is excited to be here at the amusement park also."

* "They just announced that next year's free holiday will be in Orlando. Thought of you and our conversation about someday visiting Disney World."

* "Enjoying some quality time with the family. Finally built the business to be full-time, so now we have longer weekends."

* "The young couple I told you about, John and Mary, are here with us vacationing at the park. They didn't join for the money, just for a bit more quality time with the children."

* "Thinking of you while traveling today. Hopefully sometime in the future will be a good time for you to join us in the business, as there are many more trips planned."

* "Skiing with my teenagers. Glad I am taking SuperVitamins, since now my children can almost beat me down the slopes."

* "Enjoying the view. Hope we can travel together soon. It is easier to travel with the extra paycheck to pay the expenses."

Use your imagination.

If you know what motivates your prospects, it will be easier to write that short message.

Prepare to be surprised. You might visit your prospect's home one year later and see your postcard on the refrigerator door. Yes, that postcard has reminded them about your business every time they opened the refrigerator.

Follow-up records.

What if you forget about a great prospect? What if you miss that call you promised to make?

Remove the stress of follow-up by having a simple system that works for you. The key is, it has to work for you. One type of system doesn't work for everyone.

For some distributors, a simple index card follow-up system might work. Put the prospect's name on the top of the index card, write the contact information, and make notes on what happened during the conversation. Choose a date when to follow up with the prospect, and put that card in a small box, sorted by dates to follow up.

Low-tech. Easy. Anyone can do it.

On the other extreme, some distributors might choose highly-automated software programs that sort, index, and do almost everything for the distributor except ... the actual follow-up call.

The system that you use is only a method of keeping track of who you should contact and when. The most important part is how you follow up with your prospects. A good tracking system won't make you better at talking to prospects. The actual contact is the most important thing you can do.

So use your follow-up or tracking system wisely. Spend as little time as possible on the filing, sorting, and indexing, and as much time as possible actually talking to "live" prospects.

Summary.

Remember, most of your prospects are pre-sold and want your opportunity or products. They want better lives, more money, time freedom, travel ... and all the things you offer.

By taking the attitude that your prospects already want what you have to offer, your follow-up will be more fun. You will spend your time helping your prospects feel more comfortable, helping them overcome internal objections, and helping them focus on all the good that can come from doing business with you.

Not everyone will decide instantly.

So help these people feel comfortable as you move them forward in their decision-making journey.

FREE!

Get seven mini-reports of amazing, easy sentences that create new, hot prospects.

Discover how just a few correct words can change your network marketing results forever.

Get all seven free Big Al mini-reports, and the free weekly Big Al Report with more recruiting and prospecting tips.

Sign up today at:

http://www.BigAlReport.com

MORE BIG AL RESOURCES

Want Big Al to speak in your area?

Request a Big Al training event:

http://www.BigAlSeminars.com

See a full line of Big Al products at:

http://www.FortuneNow.com

MORE BOOKS BY
TOM "BIG AL" SCHREITER

The Four Color Personalities for MLM
The Secret Language for Network Marketers

Ice Breakers!
How To Get Any Prospect To Beg You For A Presentation

How To Get Instant Trust, Belief, Influence and Rapport!
13 Ways To Create Open Minds By Talking To The
Subconscious Mind

First Sentences for Network Marketing
How To Quickly Get Prospects On Your Side

Big Al's MLM Sponsoring Magic
How to Build a Network Marketing Team Quickly

How To Prospect, Sell And Build Your Network Marketing
Business With Stories

26 Instant Marketing Ideas To Build Your Network
Marketing Business

How To Build Network Marketing Leaders Volume One:
Step-By-Step Creation Of MLM Professionals

How To Build Network Marketing Leaders Volume Two:
Activities And Lessons For MLM Leaders

Start SuperNetworking! 5 Simple Steps To Creating Your
Own Personal Networking Group

Complete list at:

http://www.BigAlBooks.com

ABOUT THE AUTHOR

Tom "Big Al" Schreiter has 40+ years of experience in network marketing and MLM. As the author of the original "Big Al" training books in the late '70s, he has continued to speak in over 80 countries on using the exact words and phrases to get prospects to open up their minds and say "YES."

His passion is marketing ideas, marketing campaigns, and how to speak to the subconscious mind in simplified, practical ways. He is always looking for case studies of incredible marketing campaigns that give usable lessons.

As the author of numerous audio trainings, Tom is a favorite speaker at company conventions and regional events.

His blog, **http://www.BigAlBlog.com** is a regular update of network marketing and MLM business-building ideas.

Anyone can subscribe to his free weekly tips at:

http://www.BigAlReport.com

Made in the USA
Lexington, KY
29 June 2016